Where the good souls dance

Selected Poetry
and Art
of

S. Abbas Shobeiri

DEDICATION

This book is dedicated to the passing breeze
and a blade of grass, in dance, unassuming.

PREFACE

When I was a child, I did not worry about what the future might hold. I just was.

I wrote frequently and I painted on whatever I could get my hands on. I generally painted on cardboard boxes with the left-over house paint in the basement. My writings and poetry were in Persian into my adulthood, through my exodus from Iran and flight into my stateless years. Consequently, this book only chronicles selected poetry written in English which became my second tongue after I washed ashore in the US in 1985.

Compiling this book, I initially started with all the poetry and quickly noticed that the volume of painful poetry written in some difficult periods of a poet's life might drive the readers to sensory overload.

I hope that the selected poetry and the art in this book are a more balanced reflection of what one's work may have to offer.

S. Abbas Shobeiri
Falls Church, Virginia, USA
February 17, 2017

Table of Content

Voices 10
Lost like Me 11
* Masks of Fate 20
The light within 22
Flashback 23
The Knock on the Door 24
Birthday 26
*Transfer 27
Frigid 28
When I Think About My Friends 29
Smooth Ride 30
Twenty-Six Mentally Ill 31
Oh God, I Repent 33
The music of tree branches 38
A Morning Loving the Earth 39
In Love 41
The loss 42
Rare moments 44
The Leaves of Mount Monadnock 46
Rubbish 47
Spider Dreams 48
A Baystate Afternoon 49
Jeremy's Factor VIII Deficiency 51
Cystic Fibrosis 55

A Seed Without a Plan	58
Chipi	59
The Touch	61
The Hunt	62
The Kite	65
*Atchafalaya Basin	66
Tourists with Bad Taste	68
*Alligator Dream	69
Running Audubon	70
Broken: Only if I Could Idle a Little	75
The Beginning	77
*Two Trees	80
Of AIDS	82
Leave the Decisions to Another Day, Again.	85
After a Phone Conversation	86
The Deer	88
Iced Tea Rabbit	89
Royal Street Shooting	90
God's Anonymous Visit	91
Under the Blue Ocean or in the Eye of the Storm	93
Every Morning's Prayer	95
*Swan of Understanding	96
Above the Clouds	98

Cigarettes	99
Not Like This	100
Petals	102
For You, I am	103
*Sunset	105
Memorial	107
Second Chances	108
Tired at the End of the Day	109
Where the Good Souls Dance	110
*The Mountain	111
The Ship of Screams	113
*Tornadoes	114
*Large Tornado	115
*Tornado on the Irish Sea	116
*Tornado and the Cross I	117
*Tornado and the Cross II	118
Beauty	119
Defiant	122
Where the Hawks Circle the Lazy Sky	126
*Skyline	128
Thump	130
Capacity	132
A sandy beach	135

*Denotes Photographs of Original Paintings

Voices

The tremors have shaken all sacred.

The fear has silenced the friends.

The fires have burnt the books.

All that embraced my soul is lost.

The ceiling floats in a circle of black clouds.

Blood rushes to my feet.

To run, to hide, to find shelter.

Trapped by the walls of existing, doing.

Shelter will be given to all at the end.

1979: In the wake of Iranian revolution

Lost like Me

In the midst of this enchanted adopted land,
with the garden of God open before me,
    I lie down
        like a naked sword
            in fetal position
    and from the furthest I hear
        the heart screeching chant of
    the broken hearts,
        unfulfilled promises.

My limits of desire to open my eyes to the
beauty before me are obscured
by a wall of knowledge.

I have learned to carry with me
cardboards of spirituality,
to sleep on
in the nights of ever-stormy assaults
under a bridge
with a drunkard or a prostitute
lost just like me.

I have learned to burn
dry bushes of my memories
through the cold days of lonely migration.

Behind these walls, nothing matters.
Free I am in my confinement.
Confined I see others in their freedom
beyond these walls
in the beauty of God.

Sitting in the downwind of memories
in the shade of strangers,
I fear the unreal peace
and the beauty of the land.

Chocked by the cloud of smoke from a
burning homeland
that hovers and surrounds only me
in any crowd.

I am of Tehran,
shaped by easy laughter
dressed by the Alborz Mountains
whose snowy slopes
the ice cream of happiness
every Friday ascend.

My brother,
jumped off the yellow school bus.
Nothing happened before this,
the earliest of my memories at age six.
An uneventful and mundane canvas,
yet to be painted on.
The memories of my unkindness towards
my brother have filled the chamber of
my subconscious sand clock.
I wish for the time to end,
for the glass chamber to break,
but with every drop of sand,
the bees of shame sting,
the fire of guilt burns,
and the vessel,

is never empty of this illusion of time.

Now I wish I was kinder
gentler to my brothers
sister and parents.

I sat in front of my house
after a school day.
Towering snowcapped Spring mountains,
train of caravans,
fresh goat milk,
bangle of golden bracelets,
brown breast tips,
Gypsy woman leaned,
     to clip a lock of my hair,
     for good luck,
          for love,
               just because.
I groomed my dogs
all happy and loyal.
It was then that my brother
jumped off the big yellow school bus.

In the Summers,
when the sun of out of school friends
          burnt carefree and warm,
I still sat quiet and content,
to remove the well-fed ticks off my dogs,
     to feed the badly ailing kittens,
to mend broken wings of terrified birds
in my basement surgery,
     to prime my childhood canvas with a
Gesso of perfection.

When I was 14,
I walked and searched aimlessly
under the gloomy sky,
ready to thunder.
Then,
the Chess game began.
There fell a Pawn.
The King with the Ray-Ban glasses,
the Queen in the white dress,
beaten, check and mate.

By age 17, predestination had reached for
me to become another little Pawn,
to move as told
to be knocked out to the sidelines.
A broken little Pawn
with a medal or two
a missing leg, an eye, or a loving wife.
That was the plan.

We gathered in the streets to face the clergy,
our new rulers,
and screamed with our loudest love
for our people.
I said,
give me a paint brush
  to fight with
  and I will unveil
  the roach of ignorance
  masquerading in the garb of religion.
Another said,
give me a pen

       to fight with,
       and I will tear out
       the worms of illiteracy
infesting the eye balls of the populous.
Intellectual voices met imprisonment,
torture and bullets.
The minds of demons saw
what they imagined:
justice, virtue, righteousness,
words in a dictionary,
not a moment of reflection.

I stood lonely
       near my innermost fears.
A giant sleeping sound cracked.
My rosy petals flew in the wind.
My marrow boiled with small thoughts.
A shade of meaning migrated to my plains.

Behind the door was by far too scary a place
for a little boy like me.

At the moment of decision,
the soul bubbled,
the unfished stream of consciousness
overflowed,
the Nile visited my eyes,
and
I saw that Spring of my life
       had had only paper flowers.

Black and white
whirling in the cup

had lost their definition.

I was lost in my own land.
Buried alive in the worms,
of war, revolution, insanity, burning,
unfamiliar surroundings,
eating at my soul.

How I listened to inner voices,
at the edge of a good deaths,
and
how I went for the search of water
of understanding,
to the edge of each well that I knew,
just to return thirstier than ever.

The well of
knowledge, dry
religion, poisoned
politics, muddy
ethics, defiled
science, walled off
innocence, raped.

I talked with my parents
softer than petunias,
more fragrant than
the seduction of knowledge.
I begged them to open their fingers
for the seed to fall.

They saw that a strange land

beyond the smoke, the chants, and the
bullets,
could be less strange,
kinder, gentler, more forgiving
for a boy like me..

My father's voice, smooth, loving,
caressed my soul:
Silence the grief of your heart.
Find those wilted flowers
      another vase.
For now there is no time.
Gather your memories to
feed you courage
for a testing journey,
unknown, unfamiliar, and at times
unforgiving.

And, I ate whole the pleasure in the solitude
of raising a sail of many colors
on the oceans of many horizons.

"Farewell home,"
I said at the start of the run.
I may never see you again.
The warmth of an imprisoned nation
betrayed
burned my skin to the depth of infinity.

My friends, my foes
our breaths were shallow
the air of terror in the skies of lies

refugees on the run.

Dusty shoes
directions without a road
whirling and untamed
roads without direction
lands without a path.

The shades raced across the lands
as the sun set
over and over again
on the horizons strange and unfamiliar.

Now
outside the windows I visit
stand my shadows of thoughts,
snowcapped Alborz mountains,
birds of the Sycamore trees,
playful children,
Gypsy caravans,
lost amid
concrete buildings
unaccustomed sceneries
unversed voices
unseen dangers.

Along the way
I hold the hands of the other refugees,
a mother, a son, or a daughter
maybe an aunt here, or a father there,
lost like me,
to lick the wounds,
to comfort,

to touch.

Sometimes I mourn with people
imprisoned by loneliness
sentenced to another unwanted life.
Sometimes I watch
mistreatment of humans
by humans that cannot feel any longer.
Sometimes I watch death,
a gasp for a last breath of air,
a last tear,
a last fear,
another leaf riding the dark sky.
And I am left not knowing,
    where their souls went.
If there is a better place after death,
    or just made up romantic notions,
    religious quotations.

We lay down in our rooms,
    and from the furthest we hear
        the heart screeching chant of
        broken hearts,
        lost just like ours,
in the midst of this enchanted adopted land
with the garden of God open before us.

1983: Bangkok, Thailand

* Masks of Fate

Masks of happiness and sadness in the foreground, facing away from of the empty barren landscape. The masks are held by the hands of fate.

This view of the snow-capped Alborz Mountains was visible from my childhood house in Tehran. The landscape was populated with trees, rivers, and life, but at the time I was painting, I could only envision emptiness. I chose to hide behind the mask of happiness in the face of the hopelessness and adversity. I became known as an "unusually" light-hearted and happy person.

The light within

A meteorite born of distant stars
      a messenger of a timeless past
      burns, flares, and hides its core.
Pure it is
      claimed by all.
           But would it fall?
      The human race, a cold storm of
despair, violence, darkness and nausea
           howls…hungers… craves for
      the warmth of the light,
         ever so quietly passing.
The tired travelling star
      a source of intrigue
           yearns to plunge and rest
                 to become a rock
      in the landscape of everyday life.
So people would not look up any longer
and instead
      seek the light within, the humanity.

Tokyo, Japan: 1984 (Translated from Japanese)

Flashback

Drawing water from an ancient well,

handing cool water to a sinned man in hell,

I watch him as he rolls in fire where he must

lay.

Memories of dark days of autumn ringing a

bell,

I help who deviously took my dignity away.

If there is a God,

let her be the prosecutor of

this heartless ail.

Seattle, Washington, 1987

The Knock on the Door

The book was sitting there,
quiet, shy and unassuming.

I opened the pages.
One word came after the other
to line-up and form sentences,
      whirlpools of twisting notions,
         crumbled pages,
            mirages in the
         desolate desert of thirst for
         something.

The words were drops of water
dripping on the dried roots of my senses,
         rejuvenated and revisited;
           emotions, laughter
      and tears
                grew.

Page after page,
the words wove
      warps and woops
         on the drawing of
someone else's life,
somewhere else,
some other time.

I read more, and the more I read
         the more I could smell
         the flowers that were
            not in the vase,

        the more I felt the still air
    and the cold light on her cheeks.

Who was this love, this lover?
another lonely soul?
        to talk to, to cry for or laugh with?
           or
        to whistle playfully in her ear?
            far from the local scenes?
            flowing cheap conversations
    and unforgettable accidents?
            night of a thousand smiles?
This book rubbed away from me all reality
    until dawn
           the land of sleep went
           ungrazed
           in a haze of clarity of words,
           deliberate sentences.

The knock on the door,
rubbed away from me all intentions
        that company, and what a kiss
                that may have been.

Bering Sea, Aleutian Islands, Alaska 1988

Birthday

A star twinkles outside.
A changing wind whistles.
A wave washes the forming icicles from the
port hole.
Gray foamy ocean rolls by,
forms valleys, mountains, and misty clouds.
A single wave, high, forbidding,
like a mad snake rushes across the valley,
and the wind chops its head off.
A seagull, not in flight,
out of control, Kamikaze,
crashes somewhere beyond the water
mountains.

I close my eyes and roll away from the
window. It must be the season.
Somewhere,
spring must be coming with flowers
     with new shoes and shirts
        for children.
Some time ago, when I was born,
     my parents must have been happy.

More waves crash against the port hole.
The boat rocks.
I close my book, turn off my head lamp
       and go to sleep.

My shift will start soon.

Somewhere in the Bering sea, Alaska 1988

*Transfer

This painting relays the story of my transfer from one fishing vessel to another in the Bering Sea. The seas were calm when we were put in the aluminum boat and placed in the water with a crane. As soon as the motor was cranked, the seas changed and a storm started to brew. The boat, not having been used for months, had taken water in the gas tank and the engine shut off between the two deep sea trawlers. Having no paddles, we desperately paddled in the frigid waters with our hands to keep our bow towards the incoming waves. The captains frantically maneuvered the fishing vessels to shield us against the waves until the engine finally gave in and started. One of the trawlers I was on sank a few years later taking many crew down with her.

Frigid

Frigid waters of the Bering Sea
stunt my fear response,
translucent blue,
deceptively calm.

Romantic notion of the smell of soil,
        bloomage of wheat,
              bread and the baker intoxicated.

Craze of long thoughts that float in my head,
the caravan of names of loved ones,
before a wave washes over me,.

Dutch Harbor, Alaska 1987

When I Think About My Friends

Where is this river going??
Under this calm surface of never knowing,
      the music of life is fast flowing.

On the shoreline of life, it is so warm today.
Footsteps on the bank,
a traveler's thirst has been quenched on her
way.
Joy floats through my veins
      unlike any other day.

Look! In the water, you see the skies.
Sky, the field of dreams in my eyes.

Plowing the river in noon high,
      searching for the light,
           a reflection of all gone by.

Exhuming retrospectively,
my plow-share flashes across the memories.

Finally, under my feet,
      there lies the globe of amity.
I kneel and reach for it, so happily.
      My fingers kiss the water.
           The image becomes a wave,
           fleeing instantaneously.
Looking up curiously,
      I have reminisced till noon high
           to find a pearl in the sky.

Boston, Massachusetts, Winter 1992

Smooth Ride

I was thinking:
    The ride has become much smoother.
    The path is covered with the leaves of
    hard gained knowledge now.
    I have travelled with the footsteps of
    experience.
    Look how well I have gained
    knowledge.
    I step in a puddle
        and fall
            as I ponder these thoughts.
    Time to shake the arrogance
            off my knees
        and patch my pride with
        humility.

Mount Monadnock, New Hampshire, 1992

Twenty-Six Mentally Ill

Twenty six sat in a circle.

Twenty seventh,

was he a schizophrenic hallucination?

"He will suffer no more,"

one physician had whispered.

"Kind and gentle he is,"

the insanes had agreed.

Physicians nodded their head judgmentally.

Silence had frightened him for

      there was much crying inside.

His visual ideation of external caring

      rarely came true.

People he saw did not hold him.

Trapped in the shell of consciousness,

In an asylum, in a dark voluntary moment

of silence by all,

    he crowned himself as God

and

    decreed the moment of his death,

    but not resurrection.

Physicians saw twenty-six,

one less,

the insanes all saw twenty-seven.

Boston VA Medical Center, Summer 1993.

Oh God, I Repent

Over the red waters, the sun rises.
      The lake, on foot, Boreas crosses.
With the wind, the dawn and the fire,
      a man's eyes romances.

"Man where are you going?"
      the breeze whispers.

"What has remained of my existence is a
stagnant lagoon.
I spend sleepless nights in the shadow of the
moon.
My life is passing its deepest dark.
What is lost within is the explosive spark.
And, this darkness enlightens the road-map
to my bereavement park.

My shadow is lost without,
and,
without a shadow
      dust has nowhere to go but to dust."

His eyebrows sitting narrow,
the man stands.
The morning stars sprinkling the clouds of
sorrow.
The man walks small among the tall grass-
field.
And the wind with its shear harvests the
yield.

"Man, where are you going?"
        shrieks the wind.

"Among all this green, there sits a tree,
lonely, a shadow!
Heaviness of mind, comes down on me,
a somber sorrow!
Brakes the confusion of dawn,
        brightness of my smile, easily,
a rainbow!
So, let me go, the morning air, for
I know!"

Now, the steep slope of the mountain under
his feet,
clouds of sun rain over the gray plains
beneath.
And the blizzard, kissing the frozen leaves
around him, shivers that,

"Man, where, where are you going?"

"I am so high!
And the sun stares at me with its hazy
morning eye.
The sun of riddles shines on her riddled son
of thought.
In such a state of mind, with the delusion of
love I may get caught.
You see?
I personally like the taste of movement,
in the current of neglect.
And, the haste of thought,

on the rocks of mistake.
My sensations,
take on the shape of any bottle,
for the liquid, limpid and fresh emotions,
not found in any brothel.
A bird in love,
a frog in sorrow,
a butterfly in pain,
a fish in distress,
will do.
If the call for affection by my love is not
true."

Hours of hike, and a freed beauty opens up
under.
In the veins of the man,
the painful time does not pulsate any longer.
To such a view any heart may surrender.
Finally, the man is sitting on a cliff.
With a nude awakening, he finds so much of
an Eagle in himself,
he feels like a thief.

"Man, where are you going?"
        the still air whispers.

"You, the morning air,
        are utterly cold.
Such a good friend,
        can never grow old.
I tried to find asylum in the world.
The loudest silence of all,
the air I have been surrounding,

like a mold.
Out of the vulnerable anxious zone I have
been living,
I laugh out loud to hear me out-loud
laughing.
In these short giggly moments, I hold,
the lead soldier in me is melt in a pot of
gold.
The green of appreciation, in such moments,
grows emphasis on the syllable of life,
I am told."

Among all these euphoric thoughts,
the man mindlessly gets up on a ledge,
gravel race him to the edge.
The stars shoot up.
The wind becomes a cradle.
And, the storm storms,
"Man..., Man..."
      it echoes.

"Like the blossom surfing the wind,
    wish I could take wing,
        on the notes of a lover,
           whose voice is softer
      than any flower.
Her lips fresh and tender as new woven silk,
    sings the inner beauty veiled by the
skin, the pearly milk.
Under a sky,
as blue as her eyes,
    I am falling until I die,
        funny that I shall be so high!!

If I am falling to my death,
oh God, I repent.
To you alone my soul can be sent.
But, if I am to become the earth,
as the indigenous claim and paint,
let a lake beat in my chest,
burning with desire
for the reflection of a forest,
whose trees are not but,
the memories of my lover
left behind.

Boston, Massachusetts, Fall 1993

The music of tree branches

It is October now.
And, I remember you, barely a friend,
bicycling alone in the woods of Middlesex
reservoir.
The music of rustling tree branches,
      wrap itself around me.
The new-found breeze,
      loves to roll in the dried leaves,
and remind me of the child
that jumped out of you in the fall foliage
in the same woods, by the same lake.

By the time the bitter cold winds take me,
I would not have known you any better.
Simple and honest,
      you have chosen to be,
           a riddle disturbing the mind,
dancing in the woods of
      the Eastern Atlantic.

Boston, Massachusetts, Winter 1993

A Morning Loving the Earth

The bowl of my eyes,
        filled with the morning light,
                overflows into my soul.

Then, you,
        rain on my roof.
And the playful child in me
        races every drop to your deepest blue.

Full of expectations, there he sits, waiting.
I say shyly:
        "Hello,
        I am the youngest expression of your
        being,
        the most perfect canvas for a painter.

        And, you,
        'a grasshopper leaped into my field of
        sadness,'
        the hopeful colorful painting of my
        hopes and dreams,
                stand
                      guard of my happiness."

By your gentle touch,
my palms are impregnated
with the seeds of hope.

As my innocence undresses in your soil,
   purified with fresh rain water,
     your somnolent green
     grows a new beginning.

The misty morning dew
   has arrived.

Your cool velvety breeze
   spreads its wings
     over my face.

I close my eyes again and stretch.

   "In the midst of the darkest,
     I have seen the clearest."

Boston, Massachusetts, Spring 1993

In Love

    The spring breeze,
            blows from the West.

    The picturesque flowers
            cry dew in their nests.

    The nectar of time
        has been put to the test,
in the veins of the lovers,
        clothed with the foliage's
                  best.

Springfield, Massachusetts, Spring 1994

The loss

Making sure not to step on the weed,
The stranger asked the children in play,
who knew where the time had gone.

Follow the Swallows, one said; and
on the edge of loneliness,
where the tears and the smiles meet,
you will find a tree.

When the sun first rained sweet rays
on the green,
a shy young tree, leafless and tender,
its trunk had endured the secrets of none.

The Spring
        seduced the tree,
            sprayed butterflies on its shoulders.

The tree rejoiced and wore a gown of
a thousand white blossoms.
A worthy bride under
the rain and gloomy sky.
She looked around,
but the Spring was gone.
The memories stood still,
Waiting, waiting in the summer sun.

Take your shoes off and climb,
to touch the winds of disappointment,
regret, and sorrow...

Follow the Swallows, another said.
    But,
        "don't remind the lone tree"
            across the purple sky
                that the butterflies are gone.

The tree is widowed with the cloak of
Winter shrouding its horizons.

Comfort the tree that another spring, in time,
will come.

Cambridge, Massachusetts, Summer 1994

Rare moments

Let us take our books
where we hear molecules collide,
where the Deer of deep thought
        need not to hide.

The busy gives and takes of daily life aside,
let's not rush through the God's garden
        with senseless pride.

If God gave me a choice on where
        I shall reside,
        between this world and the other
which to pick as my bride,
          the Earth will win my favor
        with an easy stride.
But, meanwhile, by her rules I shall abide.
        And, with the fascination of creation
be occupied.

Maybe, sit by the ocean after a tide,
        in the breeze of Dandelions
        gone for a ride,
    or, in the shadows,
    where the sun likes to hide.

With the earth-shaking sound of silence
deified,
        such moments are indeed rarefied.

With my time at this stop on a strict slide,

      let's learn the closed book God had
to provide.

Realizing "having left with no name left
behind is a suicide,"
      the urge for learning is
supernaturally amplified,
           as I sit under a tree,
              by a river,
                  paging
              through my book,
                      calmly
                pacified.

Such moments are indeed rarefied.

Boston, Massachusetts, Summer 1993

The Leaves of Mount Monadnock

My friend
and I
Look down from Mt. Monadnock.
The velvety leaves of autumn,
The last breeze of survival,
At the nature's fire,
Going out,
Mossy smell,
Tranquil sight,
Smooth to touch,
The colors of which,
Painters dare not to brush,
But with monotonous white
Pouring on our lives time after time.
Under this onion layer of
Frozen crystals, the laughter of
Leaves challenges the depths of
The inverted sky above.
Defiant they sound,
Still.

New Hampshire, Autumn 1993

Rubbish

No unfulfilled promises,
    for me.

The cats that say loud meow,
    not me.

The dogs from broken homes,
    for me.

Some call this rubbish,
    may be.

Boston, Massachusetts, Fall 1993

Spider Dreams

The house is quiet.
A familiar smell echoes in the room.
      I follow the long strands of Spider
web to find the source of smell.
There lie on the floor, a fly, laughing at me.
      Wrapped tightly in the web, but
distinctly, laughing at me.
Another flies through the cracks, right into
the web.

I am lost in the roomy memories.
      Flies are lost in time, but
      my dream is sated with their smell
      to the point of stagnation.
      I feel entangled and wrapped in their
smell to the point of suffocation.
There is always yesterday's fly
in my soup of memories.

I crawl to you,
my source of heavenly inspirations.
      You are passed out with a smile,
      wrapped in your own dreams,
      maybe of bees and honey,
      sweet smells
            and more pleasant creatures,
      you are beyond time and space.
I race you to sleep,
      May be I can catch some honey too.

Boston, Massachusetts, Fall 1993

A Baystate Afternoon

I had gone just so far
  from the truth,
    when my path crossed
      with monologue of understanding.
My eyes wide-open,
the mind, exhausted, blank,
    in a cubic room.
Golden, ruby, sapphire rainbow neck-ties,
a white medical student jacket,
set in the background of
left-over microwaved Mexican Burrito,
a paper dish,
soldiers of discipline,
the impulses of neurons from my brains
    interrupted chaotic music of disorder,
Pediatric books under my feet,
    a bag-pack distorted underneath,
leaky roof spots,
a carpet's open foul smelling mouth,
    thirsty for a decorator,
horizontal icicles,

against the cracks of the window,
> butterflies of thoughts
>> reluctant to sit on any singular subject.

Frozen blood,
> slowed down to

the pulse of seconds on my hand-watch.

Lets migrate to warmer places,

where my sadness can dry out
> in the sunny memories.

I press the earphones

heavily on my consciousness,

like a junkie's large bore needle

pour Bob Dylan's music in my veins.

My spiritual deficit,
> Uncorrectable.

The controversy of waking up,
> too sick to dance.

Maybe,
> it is time I made a house-call
>> to my home.

Baystate, Massachusetts, Fall 1993

Jeremy's Factor VIII Deficiency

When you were born,

there were neither a cloud

nor a thunder.

There were no chords plucked in the

heavens,

      to warn you.

Those eyes,

full of doubt and expectations,

cast a deep shadow into my fears.

You stare up into my face

as if I am a vampire.

You stare to face me down,

to shames me.

How wholesome are your tears

as the needle punctures the skin.

Agonizing melancholy

    draws near

as the essence of our emotions

tumble down into a single pool of

understanding.

Those large blue terrorized eyes

measure the red tube of blood.

perhaps inadequately filled.

I give a bitter smile,

raise the triumphant red candle of

knowledge.

The nurses leap to their feet

    dance in,

        like flowers,

    purple, orange and yellow scrubs.

I must step out,

let the cool air sanitize me.

The reflection of the Charles River

        brushes against my cheeks

    and dances with the wall.

Honest cruelty,

apprehensive melancholy,

unbearable breathing,

in a sanitized impersonal hospital room.

Drawing your blood,

after the tenth time,

has become a way of salutation.

Me, a happy medical student,

with another successful draw.

You, a child, unhappy,

    living one sunset at a time.

Boston Children's Floating Hospital, Spring 1994

Cystic Fibrosis

Mother, come to me.

At my face, pale is

the genetic concept of the other children's

fun,

DNA made of laugh, want, take and run,

shattered by the shake of the therapist's

palm.

Remember? The thriving stream of youth,

you labored,

endured for a screaming innocence,

a musical entry?

My eternal appreciation Mother.

For if it were not for you,

another "puff" of laughter,

a new magenta color in the sunrise,

a big glass of milk with maybe a cookie,

was not for me.

When you hear no cry from me,

come cautiously to help or follow,

I have become a fallen willow.

I know,

without my fire,

your heart is hollow.

Burn me as you desire.

Lead the way and I will follow.

For if it were not for you

I was not.

New Orleans, Louisiana, Winter 1994

A Seed Without a Plan

"I wish I could help,

but I don't want to be called paternalistic,

                    overwhelming ...".

Something is intriguing about

        a seed without a plan.

Shiny be my tomatoes.

        Purple be my eggplants.

Dust has sat on your seeds.

        When would the unicorn of dreams

arrive?

A gray hair

        sprouts.

New Orleans, Louisiana, Winter 1994

Chipi

My friend and I
walked years and years of green
in friendship, so thick and flooded.

Things we saw on the earth.
She was great, and she was real,
related to all the horizons open,
understanding the dialect of water and wind
so well.

Her voice,
the shape of a cantor of truth,
her hair,
the road to each pulse of molecules
in ever disarray.
And of her dark eyes
which turned the pages of air
in the land of honesty,
so that maybe
kindness would emigrate toward us.

The shape of quiet in her image
had travelled the loveliest corners of time,
translated into the mirror of acceptance.

And she, in the manner of the evening rain,
was full of freshness of repetition.

And she, in the manner of the majestic trees,
wished to kiss the shy face of the sun.

My childhood called in the wind
and,
the strings of thought snapped.
I biked in the puddle,
you rolled in the mud and laughed.

For us, one moment after another
touched the pray-stone of understanding,
so swiftly,
that our emotions stopped time,
and we became fresh
like a bucket of water, so limpid.

And, I saw how many times,
in my moments of distress or anger,
she left with many smiles
to pick reconciliation of emotions.
But she couldn't wait
face to face,
and she went to the edge of something
lying behind the patience of lights.

And, I have thought so often,
that between the ups and downs of
the pronunciation of her name,
how lonely she might become
chewing her bone all alone.

For my dog,

Boston, Massachusetts, Spring 1994

The Touch

The bird of her existence glided
like a drifting boat.
What an unexpected breeze of a friendship.

In the security of unfamiliarity,
we washed our faces
with the goodness of one another.

The mirrors of reality,
the repellant ripples of past knowledge,
in the mid-moon of many summers.
Her fearful eyes
wove dangers in the unseen.
Maybe an intention behind that bush,
or a roaring rage in the distance,
dancing demons around the fire of life.

Amid only-ness I was lonely.
Feet stuck in the quick sand of honesty,
lost in the bayous of caring,
loving,
her hands reached for mine,
the demons faded in our unity.

The feel of my pen,
a dagger,
plowing my inner wounds,
normally opposing the currents of life,
Now, drunk, tender, malleable, a love junky.

Boston, Massachusetts, Spring 1994

The Hunt

My breathing has changed
      as I search for a cloud
      to lift me from
      this sub-existence of a blank life.

I reach within myself and find
      black stones,
           black pearls,
                lines with
                      curved accents
to throw at this wide empty music sheet.

At first, my adolescent music sounds like
a few red hairs and horns,
      sexuality without a tempo,
      tangled musical notations,
           in unfamiliar
                addictive embraces.

A casual and unimportant G Clef,
      music for the worst kind of fools.
A small black ball
      falls off the music sheet,
      forms an avalanche,
           roaring,
           crushing,
           a messed-up music.
Semiquaver of a fish floats belly up.
Another note of an unwashed bowl in the
sink stinks.
The old cigarette with lipstick

mark blows away.
The breeze becomes a wind,
    the flower, a thorn,
        and the sea, a storm.
What started as a gentle note,
    now deafening,
    washes out a peaceful beginning.
A hunter steps on my head
    in the search of game.
I want so very badly to wake up,
and not to hear
    the cry of hunting dogs
        in the furthest.
I look up for a cloud
to raise me out of this crazed scene.
I can hear the morning bird songs,
    the sun must be up.
Wake up, smell the air,
    the fox of my dreams shall run.
This is the music of fears
    that does not end in fun,
    seen from the smoking
    barrel of a gun.

I migrate into the dark
    under the leaves,
    into the rivers.
    and the sea of musical notes roar.

I look for a flower
    to hide under,
    Passionate, Loving, Gentle,
    in this jungle of haphazard notes.

The sound of the soul cries to the fox,
to hide until
what penetrates the jungle of dreams
                                    is not the gun.
Run until
the train of understanding is full,
the music of kindness is resonant,
                          in the darkness.

The music is interrupted with a conundrum,
        a bold double bar line,
                an alarm clock ringing.

Boston, Massachusetts, Spring 1994

The Kite

I pray to the forces that hold you up,
for a gentle breeze,
for a smooth current of air....

There were no promises made, to be clear.

I would hold your strings.
And you would provide me joy as I watched
you soar.

To the right, left, sudden dives,
strong wind blowing.

Our pact has changed.

I am now a dancing puppet,
attached to your strings.

There is no shadow,
              no respite,
                          no rest.

I seek firm footing as the kite dances me.

I pray to the forces that hold you up,
              to be kind, to be gentle.

New Orleans, Louisiana, Summer 1994

*Atchafalaya Basin

Driving from New Orleans to Lafayette in the early hours I was mesmerized by the beauty of the colors that sunrise created new each day.

Tourists with Bad Taste

Sliding on the muddy mirror,
        no thunderstorms arise,
            like it should
                usually in the afternoons.
The bayou is challenged by many forces,
        subtle and fierce.
A cricket laughs in the face of quiet.
A dragon-fly, a soldier of rainbow colors,
sits on my nose,
as the hover craft pushes past the
marshlands.

Shy and so effortless, pale snowy egrets,
        fly away, into the purity of green.
I smile sluggishly, at a future that they
would like to avoid.
I lower my gaze at the boat,
        they shriek, throw chicken pieces,
and snap pictures....
Some tourists had the bad taste to wear
Alligator shoes and bags.

Not hungry,
I turn my back to rest on the shore,
in the lazy Louisiana Sun.
The boat slowly moves, disappointed,
and brakes the muddy mirror.

Alligator Annie Swamp Tours

New Iberia, Louisiana, Fall 1994

*Alligator Dream

I was in Lafayette, Louisiana and I dreamed of being a hunter in the sky. The rocks coming through the sky-water were stars and I had to navigate through alligator constellations. I woke up to paint the dream. So, I am not sure how the dream ended.

Running Audubon

Yet again,
I am in a different city.
Porches are painted unfamiliarly.

In mid-December,
when a single grass blade
broke under my feet,
by the muddy pond,
      by the foraging ducks,
       by the majestic oak trees,
      by the laughter of children,
      by the joggers in flow,
       by the giggling teenagers,
      by the playing dogs,
       by the mighty Mississippi River,
the smell of bleeding grass was so fresh,
that held onto my senses
      and filled the broken spaces
           that had always surrounded me.

I knelt and smelled the familiar scent of the
grass, the ground.

Where are the loved ones now?

After all these years,
do teenage girls of Tehran still squat and tie
tall spring grass blades
to wish for a handsome husband?
Do children still betray rumors of wishes
      the girls make?

Standing by the Mississippi River,
the stream of my childhood memories
      run serenely,
           run still,
into the subconscious of all beings.

My memories go …
      into a forest,
      into an ocean,
      into the rain.

My memories must have evaporated,
      where the quiet of the Alborz
      mountains cultivated a storm.

My memories must have rained
      in New Orleans,
      on the Mississippi River
      by Audubon Park.

Quietly I sit by the bleeding grass blade,
and get closer
to smell, to touch,
      my parents,
      my ancestors,
      the invaders,
      the takers,
      the givers,
      the beginning and the end.

The rain drops fall where I feel
      the origins of the universe.
      It washes over me.

I lean over to smell the wet ground again.
I wonder at the mystery of this
single grass blade that invites
 the wind, the water and the sun.
The mystery that invites me,
       to be here,
            now,
                    ever constant.

I see a fire-ant that holds
all the wonders of the universe.
I am at awe by the beauty of the ant
as it stings me,
spreads poison throughout my body,
and together we ascend
        to the tip of this broken grass blade.

I sit and think if it was cold,
       I could hope for frozen tears,
       to mourn,
       all the grass blades
       that I ever stepped on.

It was by this muddy pond
where the care-free old oak trees'
Spanish moss surfed the breeze.

It was here
that I crawled into crevasses of
every leaf,
       every insect,
            and every movement,

        sated with the promises of the
        past, present and the future.

It was here, in this place
that my roots ran deep and tangled
with the roots of the trees,
        the grass, the shrubs,
        that stood still, serenely.
Our roots reached the roots of all beings,
the roots of the clouds and the stars.

Our roots spanned to where there were
        no promises,
        no achievements,
        disappointments or failures.

Our roots ran deep to where there were no
        loved ones,
            parents,
                ancestors,
                      invaders,
                pride or prejudice.

We found each other,
        the rain-drops,
        coalescing in Audubon Park,
        running into the forests,
            past the past,
            a river without an agenda,
            beginning or an ending.

We became the religion that flowed
        so quietly,

so limpid,
into a horizon where
there was
> neither light,
> nor darkness,
> nor laughter,
> nor suffering.

New Orleans, Louisiana, December 1994

Broken: Only if I Could Idle a Little

I hold her hand
and look into her opaque eyes,
as she takes her last breath.

So futile my efforts,
so dismal my knowledge.

The turquoise blue and the generous clouds,
so beautiful any other day,
are the most discomforting background
any artist could paint in my mind
today.

If only I could remember
one moment of laughter,
like a spark in the dark.
Maybe then
the explosive forces of life could ignite
again.

Capsized,
not even the most desperate
would dare to ride this broken vessel.

With such a stagnant soul,
where is a wave of love,
to wash me?

Where is the breeze of a friend,
to carry me
into the sea of light?

My luster is shy of the dreams
beholding tomorrow.

Any spread of my sail to invite memories,
flags only broken promises.

Across the northern horizons,
autumn is marching.
The veins of maple trees pulsate slowly,
for the nectar of life has slowed its flow.

I have been dealt enough blows to know,
this is not the end,
just a harsh winter,
setting in.

Dying patient,
New Orleans, Louisiana, Fall 1994

The Beginning

There was a tree,
growing in the distance,
    like a hand.
A shining spark,
    in the dying and desolate land.

There was a traveler,
    a tired migrating bird,
    coasting toward the tree,
    on the rushing currents of sand.

I arranged my feathers,
    to descend
        on a branch farther.
Where there is a tree,
    you can be sure to find water.

My source of shadow
dripped the wholesome morning dew.
A young tree with wounds not too few.
A testament to the other passersby
    who never knew,
        how to love a tree,
            they had no clue.

She was an elegant tree,
the mother of a thousand vigorous leaves,
    a thousand stories to be explored.
Beyond the healed surface,
were a thousand blows to the heart,
        never to be told.

A bird and a tree,
      a fairy tale that could hold.
A bird and a tree,
      nature in harmony,
           that was very bold!

One blow to the heart,
      may never heal in entirety.

A thousand blows to the heart of a tree,
      could only be eased
      by the nest of a bird
           who was flying free.

In a universe full of life,
the bird decided to have this tree for a wife.

This beautiful tree with a bird
      was more beautiful now,
           it was not hard to see how.

To complete the circle of life,
      the bird burned all its feathers
      and wished for an egg of destiny.

The tree cried at the sacrifice
and protected the egg until its own demise.

The tree's sorrow and loss
      perfused the egg of paradise.

Soon, a sapling sprouted
>through the shell,
>and the heavens sounded
>>with joyous bells.

They were one now,
>the tree and the bird,
>>in music and harmony.

They spread seeds,
that bore
>the sky,
>the clouds,
>the mountains and even streams.

Some other seeds they kept
>in a nest full of golden dreams.

For Eileen, New Orleans, Louisiana, Fall 1995

*Two Trees

This painting for Eileen, was inspired by poetry of Kahlil Gibran on marriage in his book, The Prophet.
"Give your hearts, but not to each other's keeping.
For only the hand of life can contain your hearts.
And stand together yet not too near together:
For the pillars of the temple stand apart,
And the oak tree and the cypress grow not in each other's shadow."

Of AIDS
Bissant and five others,
    too much alike,
        lie in a room.

He was quiet.
And, he was shy.
A young man with a gigantic Afro,
    not ready to die.

He would have been a teacher,
    if it was not for "the disease."

No one knows what it is or
Where it came from.
Some say it is a plague,
The vengeance of God,
On the adulterous, gay and impure.

Bissant, straight and pure,
day after day asked me, "Doc?"
Is it too much to ask?
A piece of pizza,
a little sunshine
under which I can marry my woman?

Answer my question, Sir!
If you cannot breathe,
Shall we stick a tube in your throat?
Shall the machine breathe for you?

Think about it, Sir!

If your heart does not beat,
Shall we shock your heart?
Shall we pump on your chest?

Make an informed decision, Sir!
If you become unconscious
it will be your mother,
left with the burden of your fate.

Six lie in a room,
        Six die in the room.
              too much alike.

They lie in their beds,
        afraid of sleep.
,
Bissant looks at me,
        with a black lesion on his head.
His voice painfully slow, labored,
        a stopping train.

"God, Doc,
        the woman of my dreams,
        if only there was one.
        And a slice of pizza.
        Is it too much to ask Doc?

I hold his hand,
Not knowing if he is contagious.
The tears pool in my mask,
steam my face shield.
His face close to me,
his breath perhaps deadly to my body,

washes over me,
sanitizes my soul.

Bissant,
Close your eyes
and imagine,
having lived a full life,
many pizza dinners with your wife,
many children to celebrate,
many walks by the ocean,
many triumphs and trials of old age.
If you could not breathe,
if your heart fluttered,
What would you want your family
surrounding your bed to decide?

He barely had enough strength to give me a
bitter smile,
closed his eyes,
holding my hand,
his breaths now shallow, rasping,
disappearing,
his heart now fluttering, stopping, fluttering,
a flat line on the monitor.

The grip loosened.
I held his hand for the longest time.

AIDS ward, Charity Hospital,
New Orleans, Louisiana, Winter 1995

Leave the Decisions to Another Day, Again.

The silk shirt or a wooden clog?
The jump of a deer or the leap of a frog?

The muddy waters or the transparent sea?
The song of a lovebird or a bumble bee?

The emptiness of the skies,
    or the fullness of storm?
Choosing defiantly,
    or following the norm?

The bells of a church,
    or the song of cantor?

Rescuing the world,
    or committing to none?

Differences that divide us like the open sea,
    scream in me:
    "Let me be, please let me be."

Pros and cons collide on my grounds,
meanwhile,
wounded I am,
dreaming of a sleep,
        sound.

*Tulane University Hospital, New Orleans, Louisiana,
Winter 1995*

After a Phone Conversation

It seems,
she has chosen this to be her playground.

The tree, the swing, the quiet,
and the serenity seem so lovely.

The tree's presence is
        clean, pure, and wholesome.
No spider of opinions or judgements hide
        in this inviting shade,
        in this sanctuary.

She doesn't notice his battered bark,
        many times broken branches,
                many times used for play.

She swings like a pen that draws
        painful memories
        in the purity of his shadows,
        fresh writings on the trunk.

Every time she leaves,
        the wounds are left smarting,
                so much.

For the tree, each of her movements,
        hold the smell of ozone,
        fear of the lightening to come,
        fractured limbs.

His story,

   his screaming silence,
      lost in her gathering storms.

She frequently leaves,
   livid at the quiet of the tree.

She doesn't hear when the leaves fall,
   the branches snap,
     as she swings,
     and falls,
     wounded
   in her very usual way.

She goes on her way,
   leaving him sad,
   yearning,
   for the tender touch of a gardener
   who can heal his wounds
   who can understand.

Baton Rouge, Louisiana, Winter 1995

The Deer

When the day is new
        the joys so few,
watching the deer that go by,
makes my heart soar
        like a balloon in the sky.

There is a river,
        a current.

There is an ocean,
        a wave.

Hunters are near,
hidden in the shadows.

Slippery ground under her feet,
        the air drifts,
        the shadows move,
        hesitance runs wild.

The calf watches in the distance,
        never knowing,
        why the river ran red,
        or why the ocean roared.

Hartford, Connecticut, Winter 1995

Iced Tea Rabbit

My iced tea smells like my brown bunny.
       She groomed herself as I left.

On the road to Charity Hospital,
up the ramp,
there was nothing between me and the sun.
The clouds were shaped like hopping
bunnies.

I sip some more of my tea.
She leaped high and snapped her back feet.
Light brown, fist sized, emotionally stable.

Empty New Orleans' streets before a storm.

I close my eyes,
to welcome the warm wave of numbness,
re-living the contentment
when I hold my rabbit.

New Orleans, Louisiana, Summer 1995

Royal Street Shooting

Alertness of thoughts,
a substitute actor of my aloof character,
hears only quiescence
in the midst of Royal Street,
where the little bullets broke
many sleepy spectators' romantic notions.

In the midst of the street lies
the empty coffins of shells,
golden keys to a moment of awakening.

The moment of confused smiles is touched
as the empty air of disbelief is grasped.

The hair of death,
blown intermittently
into the passersby's faces.

Only if some blood was shed tonight
would the dust of indifference within
lift in reaction.

New Orleans, Louisiana, Fall 1995

God's Anonymous Visit

When God stepped on this Earth,
      her emotions were deeply hurt,
      for she had landed in a pile of dirt.

One screamed:
This is no place for a woman to be!!
The bars are the seeds of male fleshly
ecstasy.

Since this visit was arranged anonymously,
      she was thrown into the street
      unceremoniously.

Aimlessly, one foot followed the other,
      to find ruined,
      what was created beautiful rather.

There slept a child in a pool of blood,
      Did your father do this to you?
            The girl died with a nod.

Outraged by all this,
she took her complaints to a church!
Just to find the priest molesting
      God's children on the bench!

She passed poor people holding on their
back a Golden mosque at high cost!
What she had perceived as an extravagant
plan had turned into dust!

Her elder son, Moses,
she thought may be home!
Instead she found his nation
              in the hopes of conquest
                  from Mesopotamia to Rome!

She had given her light to the world.
In darkness she sat, feeling quite cold.

Pondering quite lonely:

    "Among all these people,
    if I could find One person only,
    worthy of my imminence,
    in the house of Glory.

    She whose heart IS the paradise,
    not all who seek heaven,
    for fear of demise."

New Orleans, Louisiana, Winter 1997

Under the Blue Ocean or in the Eye of the Storm

When you scream I become sad.
I hold my breath
       and close my eyes
       waiting
       for the moments to pass.

I can see, but not hear
the storms of anger
as the overcast sea of emotions
       drowns me.

As I sink,
the floating hair pulls on my head.
The inverse reflection of the sun
invites the tiny bubbles to the race of unity
with the sky.

I wish for the sea of blue to caress my mood.
For now, the oscillating calm and fury,
is the mistress sharing my bed.

In such suspense of quiescence
I sink swiftly
to the tranquil bamboo forest of memories.

At the horizon of contemplation,
the heat from the fire of unkind words,
unspoken jests,
still burns as my tears drown me.

Unrelenting intense words,
that burn more,
each time they wound me.

Numb to the words that are now only words,
used so much,
until they have lost their meaning.

How I hunger for a kindness
greater than reason would allow.

For now, I anchor my thoughts
in the bamboo forest of memories
and let the storm of unkind words
                                      pass…

Lafayette, Louisiana, Winter 1997

Every Morning's Prayer

I open my pen
to send you the swans of understanding
for greeting.

If my eyes were the sea,
> you were the guiding light at nights.

If I spoke of flowers,
> you were the meaning and the depth.

If I painted a landscape,
you were the sun breaking through the
clouds.

If a tear rolled down my cheeks,
falling like the morning dew,
it did so,
as my soul was yearning for you.

If you think that I can't describe you,
or
digest you intellectually,
  Forgive me!

Do I sing like a Partridge
lost in the aroma of the Spring?
How would I know?
What are my prayers or songs for?

God gave us fire for warmth not burning.
She gave us love for joy not yearning.

New Orleans, Louisiana, Winter 1997

*Swan of Understanding

I was teaching my daughters how to paint with a knife in horizontal continuous strokes. Swan of Understanding, is the love, kindness and passion for one another on the flow of gliding yet at times turbulent, moments.

Above the Clouds

You
have not seen the unseen,
yet you can envision me clearly.

You
have not heard the dreams,
yet you are the tail of the rainbow,
the legacy of a shooting star.

We
are the absolute,
your desires and burdens,

You are everything.
You
are the mirror of the heart,
the reflection of light.

" I "
is only because of you
separate for now.

Believing in me,
is believing in
it,
which bonds our distance.

Baton Rouge, Louisiana, Summer 1999

Cigarettes

Life is a cigarette.
  And, it causes lung cancer.
It causes unhappiness.
  It is smoked before your eyes.
And, it causes your skin to loosen and hang from your body.
  It makes others around you uncomfortable.
It is delicious as it burns away.
Yet, it has the yellowing effect on your teeth as they loosen and decay.
  It makes you age.
It induces your bones to crumble under your weight.
Life can be a cigarette or a candy,
both bad for you.

New Orleans, Louisiana, Fall 2000

Not Like This

Clump, clock, clump, clock, clump …
Driving concrete roads
Moving ahead
The road narrows
Louisiana welcome center is near.

Clump, clock, clump, clock, clump …
One less clump
One less clock of the road
One second less to home
One second closer to loved ones.

How eager I was
To arrive in New Orleans.
Then,
one pearl of a tear rumbled down
for
it was such a beautiful day to die.
But
not like this,
without a wife to hold his hand,
a child to feel his fainting pulse,
a mother to hear the last efforts of his
collapsing lungs.

Not
with the towers of fire tumbling down,
in our minds,
over and over again…
for each floor a gasp,
for each gasp an ocean of spirits,

drained from our lives.

Now,
the hands are searching the rubble for
other hands.
Bands are hunting the world for other bands.

Although
revenge is still sleepy these smoky days
the rules of behavior have crumbled down.

In these days of terror, burning hopes,
in these hours of decay and lonely calls
from the air pockets,
trapped,
below the shaken earth in the sky.

Torn to pieces
mixed with the blood and filth of
the hunters,
inseparable taste of life and death,
temple of death, raided,
molested, left bleeding,
our sorrow, desecrated.

There is never a good day to die,
not like this.

New Orleans, Louisiana, in memory of September 11, 2001

Petals

Pink, blue and white petals,
dance in the hands of the wind.

River of passing Aristocrat pear trees.

Year after year.
The same sunny day, the same direction,
the same force.

If anything,
I would have wanted more:
Cherry blossoms, cotton candy, State Fairs.

I am sailing in the wind.

Let my fruits be sweet.

Their days filled with:
Cherry blossoms, cotton candy, and Spring affairs.

I have felt the breeze picking up in my direction.

Oklahoma City, Oklahoma, Summer 2002

For You, I am

You,
sleep on the wings of the angels,

And I,
staring at your lips,
pulsate as an element of you,
feeling the leap of the morning-dew drops,
sensing the awaking smiles,
believing the vibration of the moments.

I offer you the swan of understanding,
battered, hardened, yet innocent,
wings tied at your submission.

In the stormy nights,
I am afraid,
and hear
the rain against the window.

If I see gray skies,
I feel so alone,
and release
the warm tears that I wipe quickly.

In the hours of confusion,
I abandon my heart,
and renounce
the thought of flight.

If I see a distant rainbow,

I close your eyes,
and hope
the dream of love and emotions will pass.

Open your heart and let
your swan of understanding sail out
where I await,
to wrap necks,
to feel whole just for a short while.

Come to me where
I wait for the other storms,
the other gray skies,
more confusion, and
maybe a rainbow.

I am singing to you in silence,
and in silence,
go to sleep on the wings of the angels
content and secure.

Oklahoma City, Oklahoma, December 2003

*Sunset

This painting depicts the ascent of our souls to the heavens. The painting can be hung either with the golden side up or the black side up, depending on your point of view if heaven is dark or light. Most viewers see this painting as a sunset.

Memorial

Where the mountains hesitate in the winds,
where the clouds weep,
close to the knowledge of God,
fallen stand,
hand in hand,
their presence
eternal, palpable.

On the towers built of their bones,
there is nothing said about cries,
children, or wives,
enduring their memories.

There is nothing said of defeat or poverty,
hope or abundance.

The creamy blossoms that never fall,
the breeze of memories
move the trees to paint the sky,
golden lights that bathe
the green-black clouds
menacing the horizon.

Culloden Moor, Scotland, Summer 2011

Second Chances

Yes,
I have had a few moments in my life,
when I was here:
Ascending the veins of love through my
parents' touch.
Drowning in every molecule of
                            Eileen's eyes.
Dipping fingers in paint with my children to
become what we painted.
Wandering in my friends' direction
                            until I lost myself.
Giving joy to the orange cat lying on my lap
until I became the purr.

But most often, I have been
the background noise,
a dispensable sentence,
a sub-title to a bad movie,
believing that there would be
                            a second chance.

I have simply been a spark of darkness
dancing immiscibly on the unreachable,
                            vast ocean of light.

Oklahoma City, Oklahoma, Fall 2011

Tired at the End of the Day

The head hangs low.
        The breathing is slow.

Fire burns under your feet
        The air smells of defeat.

Eyes cloudy,
        actions slow,
                reactions slower.

Hello…Hello…Hello….

My voice echoes.

The smile is tired.
The hair, the eyes, the lips still smell the same.

Mother's Day is near.

Where can I find feathers for a long flight
into the cage of memories?

Edmond, Oklahoma, Spring 2013

Where the Good Souls Dance

Some say,

the days and nights will dissolve,

    the tides will wash the moon,

        the majestic mountains will shake,

  and

the mighty oceans will bleed,

    when you awake.

    I can feel you not far, ever.

I say,

    Hop on my knee,

        as a grasshopper,

    beautify the world,

        as a rose,

    sanitize my soul,

        as a breeze.

Or simply be,

    where the good souls dance.

Edmond, Oklahoma, November 2014
In memory of a friend.

The Mountain

One of my older paintings shows the continuity of life in light blue lines through the Earth and the Sky. The small "beings" in the bottom of the painting coalesce into like colors on their path to perfection, symbolized as a seemingly unreachable snow cap in the midst of clouds of light and darkness.

The Ship of Screams

Beyond these oceans
    there may be a dream.
Chance boarding,
    the disturbed ship of screams,
        rolls among the foamy waves
        of temptation.

The screams, chain the emotions,
    redundancy of thoughts,
        confused entanglement,
        delusion of a happy life.

Guiding stars,
    lost in this ocean,
        sails open,
        what dreams do you seek?

Wrapped in confusion,
    the dream you find
        escapes....

Edmond, Oklahoma, Spring 2014

***Tornadoes**

When I found out my nurse of 13 years had lung cancer and was dying, something in me broke. I started sketching and painting many tornadoes, when the subject had not interested me before. Their sudden emergence through a serene landscape must have resembled Lea's sudden diagnosis. From the time of diagnosis to her death in November 2015, which was about six months, I sketched more than 50 tornadoes and painted five.

*Large Tornado

This wall sized tornado on a large canvas (about 9 feet diagonal) was painted throughout a month-long period while the smaller tornadoes were painted when I needed a rest from the big canvas.

*Tornado on the Irish Sea

The serene recollection of an Irish seaside scene was disrupted by this tornado.

*Tornado and the Cross I

My nurse's faith in Christ and her approaching fate were contradictions in coexistence. Here the tornado is showering the Cross with raining fire.

*Tornado and the Cross II

Beauty

I have turned in
 my badge,
  my hat,
   my holster
   and my ultrasound probe.

  Never got around to getting a horse.

This town needs to find itself
 another Sheriff.

The people of this town are made of
   love and dust.
Their land rolls in that very gentle way.
Bountiful be their harvests....
  Greener be their greens...
  Ever-flowing their kindness....

In the distance,
there is thunder
which pulls our lives into inviting shadows.

In the distance
there is the ozone of memories
that sates the senses.

Here, there are melancholy of smiles,
  fatigue of the heart-beats,
  and the hesitance of steps.

The roots have run, hidden, dug

       in unexpected places,
       unknown dimensions.

And, as we said good-byes,
we each mourned the loss of the other.
As the others mourned one,
       we mourned the loss of hundreds.

We each wept differently,
       lost differently,
       but understood the pain the same.

The pain,
       burned,
             sawed,
                   twisted,
                         and melted
             into courage's hiding places,
       with a wave of nausea
       that recalled
       the moments of despair
       and
             more pain.

The town folks
came,
       kissed,
             hugged and comforted.
Flowers, baked bread, cards
and Facebook notes,
       dulled the pain of separation.

And, as they said their peace,

we knew that we could leave
> with the knowledge, not the hope,
> that we had made a difference.

As I handed in each piece,
> I felt my being dismantled.

As I am pulled into the storms,
> witnessing the enormity
>> and devastation of our loss,
> unfolding.

I wish for a gentle Sheriff
> who can understand
>> the beauty I have witnessed.

Edmond, Oklahoma, August 2015

Defiant

Of all the stars fixed in the sky,
        none belonged to you.

Dawn fast approaching,
      exhausted in this fight,
      we watched your labored rattles,
      heavy chest rising,
      crackles of struggle,
      breaking the intermittent cries.

The dark fog of death hovered heavy
        in the corners.
  We held hands,
      formed a wall,
          and hugged you.

The shadow now was working its dark
magic from within.
    Growl of death sinking its fangs in you,
    deafening,
        light poured out of your wounds.
        We watched you pulled down,
        dissected,
            defiled,
                violated.
        Not ready to go,
        still,
        so much left undone.

Your eyes, glassy and opaque asked,
      for the end of suffering,

for a sharp knife on the jugulars,
merciful, forgiving.

We resisted,
    cried,
        held you tight,
           hopeless.

There is never a good time
to have the courage to end a life,
to turn the oxygen off,
to say good-bye to your friend, husband,
daughter, or even a stranger.

Your heart raced, still defiant,
    and then faltered.
We prayed that now death would take you
swiftly, painlessly.
    But, it didn't.
It slowly gnawed on your bones,
flooded your lungs,
and squeezed your heart.
Your body fought,
heartbeats agonized, slowed, fought, raced,
danced, cried, begged,
and then,
    laid down as a flat line
        on the monitor.

Then, the heart beats agonized
    again and again,
slowed, again and again,
fought, again and again,

raced, again and again,
danced, again and again,
cried, again and again,
begged, again and again,
and then,
laid down as a flat line,
maybe,
for the final time on the monitor.

One with you, our hearts exhausted, ached.
Our wounds smarted.
Our lips,
     curled up,
          in a last attempted smile,
               and froze.

Our world buckled, broke;
               scared without you.

Exhausted of the fight, we looked up,
our world dark with the haze of sadness,
          with the smoke of emotions.

The corpse of your memory hangs
     from the tree of our loneliness,
     swinging in the breeze of life,
     telling the observers of our agony
     and sorrow.
          Forcing us to tell
          our story
          that once you were here.
          Forcing us to vomit
          this poison,

        this foul experience.

The burning tar of grief is stuck to our
deepest beings.
        Heavy with our experiences,
        now and then,
        it burns,
            smolders,
                smokes,
        in the most unexpected times,
        and unexpected places.

Falls Church, Virginia, November, 2015

Where the Hawks Circle the Lazy Sky

I lean into the dark, listening,
for my daughters, downstairs,
with hearts, heavy from the fog of departure.

What is to fish for in the sleepy dimensions?

Peaches pure,
Cottonwood white, and
Blues wide and innocent,
as lonely as,
where the hawks roam,
above the red roof
of an empty house.
Where dreams are
locked in another time and dimension,
and the urgency of dreams
does not fade in the stagnation of thoughts.

My daughters wake up sometimes
saddened by their reveries.
They yearn for the sound of thunder,
the howling wind,
and the Spring hail.

Now, they hear
the song of blue jays,
the cry of foxes,
and sometimes
the kiss of the shore by a wave...
unwelcomed, unwanted, uninvited.

I sing them to sleep,

"Wherever you are
be the bear that dreams unlike any other,
climb the life distinct from another.
Don't dream,
be the dream of the drunken thirst of life."

So thick the blood of expectation
in my veins,
slippery are my thoughts,
falling sleep in an uneasy quiet,
next to my daughters.

Falls Church, Virginia, Winter 2015

*Skyline

Painted with knife and left-over paint, this painting depicts tomb stones. Interestingly, the viewer may see a city skyline.

Thump

Once, I saw a tiger spider that fell
        from the trees
        by our house on Coltrane Road.
It fell down fast and heavy
        like hail,
hitting the ground with a "Thump" sound,
                and bounced.
As she rolled and I witnessed
        her soul fly out of her
        and disperse into hundreds of
        little pieces crawling
        all over the pavement.
She raised herself on her shaky legs,
        bruised, and mutilated,
            and gathered her babies,
        one by one,
        put them on her back,
    tediously, painstakingly,
    and carried them to safety,
while one broken leg dragged behind her.
Not a single baby spider was left behind.

Her soul and her totality restored.

I had fallen time after time in my life,
confident that I would soften any blow.
Time after time I would get up,
      shake the dust off my knees,
      and continue the course,
           unrelenting, undefeated.

But, this time it was different.
      WE fell with a Thump,
           Together.
Didn't open our arms,
      didn't let our souls fly out.
Breathless,
      bruised,
           mutilated,
we opened our arms,
      smiled,
and let our babies peak out.

Falls Church, Virginia, Spring 2016

Capacity

I hugged you,
        joked with you,
leaned on you,
        smiled at you,
simply because
 I loved you,
        and you,
                and you,
                      and you.
Each and every one of you,
bright flowers in the spring of life,
        merciful drops of light,
        illuminating my path,
                to the end.

This kindness I gave you,
you were supposed to sip,
        to drink,
        to cherish,
                not to drown in,

extinguishing your fire.

This smile I painted on your face
with my light-heartedness,
you were supposed to treasure,
    to wear with pride,
    to take to your core,
    not to examine with suspicion.

This stage I gave you,
you were supposed to stand on, to shine on,
    to enjoy the moment,
    to feel appreciated,
        not to carry on your back,
        like a mountain.

So excited I acted,
    at the sight of you,
    and you,
        and you,
            and you,
often I forgot

  that even the gentle breeze
     could wear out the rocks;
  that even the morning dew
     could dampen fires,
  and the mere light
     could wither flowers.

  So, I learned to sit at a distance,
     cautiously,
      watching you, loving you,
     and you,
       and you,
        and you…

Falls Church, Virginia, Fall 2016

A sandy beach

The island is asleep.
The music boxes are heard still
in the distance, somewhere,
although the party has ended.
With the first step, the moist sand wraps in
the hollow of my foot and invites the other.
The gentle hum of low tide
sings a lullaby.
A sliver of the moon is still visible
above the crimson skies.
A dragon-fly on the tidal pools
busy at work.
Yellow, green, red boats
moored in the bay.
Drunken lovers
sleep
in a tied-up fishing boat,
rocked in the cradling waves.
A Rum bottle rolls on the sand nearby.
articles of clothing
thrown on the fishing net here,

a rock there,

a branch in the distance.

They are passed out uncomfortably

in each other's arms,

maybe unaccustomed, unprotected, twisted,

spent, seasoned.

A few gnats feeding on their skin

produce movements.

I continue

my journey with no destiny.

By the rocky coral,

I listen to the ocean

for the longest time.

The moist sand grows into my veins,

a wave gently invites me in,

the mist hugs me dearly,

but the missing piece is not here,

not this morning.

On the way back,

the man is sleep in the boat alone,

crumpled, deserted, insignificant.

A few items of women's clothing are
missing from the tree branch,
another puzzle, unfinished.

Treasure beach, Jamaica, New Years Day 2017

Notes:

Notes:

www.ingramcontent.com/pod-product-compliance
Lightning Source LLC
Chambersburg PA
CBHW042320150426
43192CB00001B/5